THE
Archive Photographs
SERIES
CHESTERFIELD

Chesterfield High Street about 1840, from a drawing by Ashton Greene. Burlington Street was formed in 1837 and initially known as New Street. The early Town Hall is pictured extreme left and the grocer's shop, under the pillared arches, was run by George Barker, becoming well known later as the premises of T.P. Wood, wine and spirit merchant.

THE
Archive Photographs
SERIES

CHESTERFIELD

Compiled by
Roy Thompson

CHALFORD

First published 1994
Reprinted 1997
Copyright © Roy Thompson, 1994

The Chalford Publishing Company
St Mary's Mill, Chalford,
Stroud, Gloucestershire, GL6 8NX

ISBN 0 7524 0014 2

Typesetting and origination by
The Chalford Publishing Company
Printed in Great Britain by
Bailey Print, Dursley, Gloucestershire

Contents

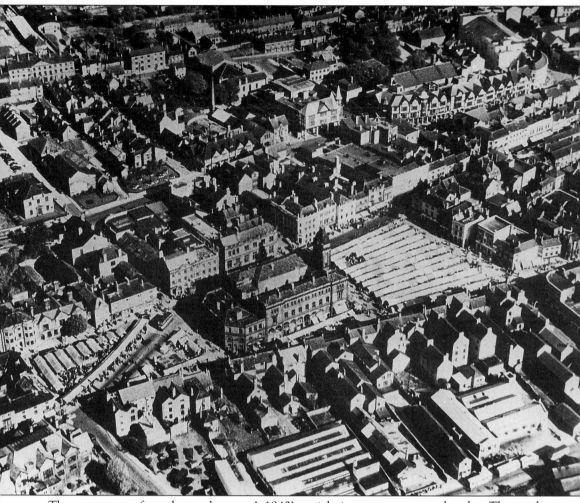

The town centre from the south-west. A 1940's aerial view on a sunny market day. The north to south disposition of the many yards can be seen below Low Pavement and the Market Place. A local nurseryman had laid out temporary gardens on Rose Hill between Glumangate and Soresby Street.

Acknowledgements

Grateful thanks are extended to all who lent, gave or otherwise supplied photographs, information or guidance for this book, in particular A. Boreman, B.W. Marsden, Mrs. E. Minter, G.J. Newman, J. Sergeant, G.G. Speed, G. Tagg, Mrs. M. Tupman, the staff of the local history section of the Chesterfield Library, the Building Control Dept. of the Borough Council, and a gentleman who wishes not to be named but without whose knowledge and help this book would have been much the poorer. And not least to my wife, without whose patience, encouragement and ability the book would not have been started.

Introduction

"A handsome, populous town, well built and well inhabited, with a good market well stocked with provisions."

So said Daniel Defoe at the beginning of the 18th. century after visiting Chesterfield. At this time, the town was, in common with most towns of its size, relatively isolated, and had little more than the trades and professions necessary to provide for its citizens. The only commodity imported in quantity was salt from Cheshire, and the only exports were lead in Roman times and wool in later years, when the town was used as a distribution point for these materials.

Real expansion of the town and area began with the Industrial Revolution for, situated virtually in the middle of England, and built on deposits of coal, ironstone and clay, Chesterfield was in a prime position to exploit these resources, and did. Great companies were established, largely on the town's periphery, which made their names nationally and internationally – in iron making (Staveley), or engineering (Sheepbridge, Bryan Donkin and Plowrights), all feeding off one another and off the raw materials so close at hand.

At the same time, as now, Chesterfield was still a market town, although the coming of the railways had brought prosperity and opened up the whole country to its products. The railway pioneer George Stephenson had founded the Clay Cross Company and settled at Tapton. The railways, of course, helped the local mining industries to prosper, not only by using their products, but by taking them swiftly to new markets.

In 1994, much of this industry has disappeared or been greatly diminished. Iron making has ceased, reducing the need for coke and therefore coal; the railways use oil, and power stations prefer gas and oil. Former suppliers to these industries, therefore, have had to look to other markets, sometimes leaving the district in order to do so.

The wheel seems to have turned a full circle, though, and now the town is busy in its new and thriving Industrial Estates, nurturing fresh industries of many kinds. It is significant that Chesterfield is now more often referred to as the "Gateway to the Peak" than the "Centre of Industrial England", and that tourism is better catered for than previously. The old town is adapting, just as it always has.

This book is primarily a look at a Chesterfield of the past, a tour of the town that a visitor might have made if entering from the south and proceeding round the streets in a somewhat logical fashion. The captions have been designed to complement the pictures, and care has been taken over their accuracy, approximations being indicated where best attempts to establish facts have failed.

Many prints have been excluded for reasons of quality or over-reproduction, and a few interesting or attractive photographs have been selected even though factual detail may have been lost. The discovery rate for "old" photographs is diminishing, depending on what is defined as old, and it is no consolation to realise that one's own photographs may one day be regarded as "old"!

Thanks are expressed elsewhere to all suppliers of pictures, but an introduction to a book of this type would be incomplete without acknowledging the photographers of these bygone scenes; if not pioneers, they left a valuable and irreplaceable record of the town of their time. Charles Harold Nadin was perhaps the most prolific local cameraman in the early part of the century, and tribute is paid to him elsewhere in this book; Alfred R Rippon was a postman from Minimum Terrace who cycled round the district with his camera; John Henry Waterhouse was a professional photographer who lived in Hadfield Town by the Queen's Park and operated a studio on Cavendish Street; Alfred Seaman was the founder of the long-lived business in Chesterfield and other towns.

One
Old Chesterfield

Maynard's Meadow, c. 1870. The other, northern, end of the house terrace on the left ended in White Horse Yard, a hostelry on the site of the present Portland Hotel. These houses, and those lying on the slopes to the east, were known as the Dog Kennels.

The Horns Bridge complex in the late 1920's. Possibly unique, the bridges carried one railway (LDEC) over the two others (LMS and LNER), two trunk roads and the River Rother. The 63ft. high viaduct comprised seven brick arches and four girder spans and was 700ft. in length.

Horns Bridge from the south, then the main road to Mansfield and Nottingham. There were several shops opposite, on the A61, the largest being that of the Jervis Brothers, motor dealers.

Demolition for road widening, 1932. Not a bulldozer in sight, all dismantling being by hand and pneumatic drills. Presumably this meant a lengthy detour for town-bound Hasland traffic.

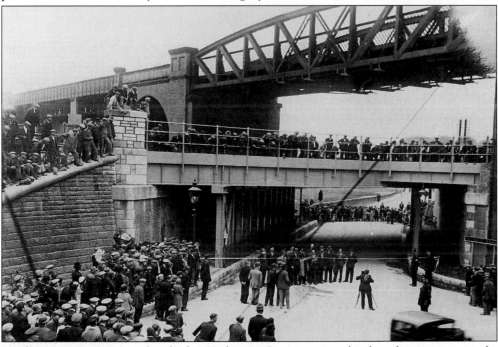

Road improvements completed, the Highways Committee and other dignitaries pose for photographs, surrounded by workmen and onlookers. The photographer must have been on the top deck of a bus or similar vantage point. The whole complex lasted from the 1890's to the 1970's.

The other gasworks. This chimney base, apart from odd foundations, was all that remained of the old coal gas plant in 1982. This small gasworks was owned by the Midland Railway and supplied gas to their rail-side lamps, signal box and the station.

The east end of Markham Road in the early 1950's. The old cottages up Lordsmill Street were removed for road widening and a large traffic island. Frisby's shoe repair depot on the corner of Dixon Road also went, as eventually did their shoe shop on Burlington Street.

Beetwell Street in the 1930's. All the buildings seen on the south side, together with the north corner, were removed for road improvements, further development being delayed by the Second World War. Hanson's saddlers was relocated in Cavendish Street for many years.

After demolition and road widening the land on the south corner of Beetwell Street was empty, bearing a sign proclaiming that it was reserved for development by motor dealers Boult & Clough. After the war, in the 1950's, Vauxhall House, offices with a garage on the corner, was built by Jack Boult but was, in turn, demolished and replaced by more offices and a bingo hall.

Lordsmill Street in the early 1930's. All the properties shown disappeared on either side of the war period. The Crown Hotel, left, owned by the Brampton Brewery, lasted until 1966, when the licence was transferred to the Badger, Brockwell. Just visible to the right of Kerslake's Pork Butchers is another Brampton pub, the Prince of Wales on Beetwell Street, which also closed in the 1960's.

Opposite: Anchor Hotel, St. Mary's Gate, 1922. The date is precise since it is on record that the Ship Inn on the other, Hollis Lane, corner was rebuilt by the Brampton Brewery at that time. The 'Cannon Ales' on the windows indicates a Stones house, and in 1923 it was rebuilt in mock-Tudor fashion like the new Ship Inn opposite. John Leivesley was the licensee at this time. The pork butcher's shop could have belonged to Samuel Hadfield, who had a shop on Lordsmill Street.

No. 11 Bath Place, said by W. Godfrey, a respected local historian, to be the smallest house in Chesterfield. Bath Place was a small enclave of perhaps twelve houses off Lordsmill Street just below Hollis Lane, one of several running at right-angles to the main road. The photograph is thought to date from about 1930, prior to demolition. The houses in Bath Place were built by a Quaker, Wm. Bingham, in the mid-19th century and this one was put in the space remaining. It was said to have been occupied by a favoured nurse in her declining years. A correspondent in the *Derbyshire Times* of 1923 states that the house was home to a family with two children in 1868, the roof space being used as a bedroom. When the husband was killed in an accident, 'Quaker' Bingham helped the widow and paid for her son to be educated at the British School in Hollis Lane.

St. Mary's Gate in 1895. The dark building behind the 'pinafored' children is the old Ship Inn, dating from 1887. The street name is something of a puzzle since it was known by its present title even when the church was referred to as All Saints'. It is one of the oldest thoroughfares in Chesterfield and was once known as Southergate, Soutergate or Churchgate. As the A61 it is still one of the most heavily used, even though the town now has an inner by-pass.

Hollis Lane in the early 1980's. This ancient thoroughfare was once known as Kalehalegate, meaning the road to Calow, but the coming of the by-pass in the 1980's changed all that, the road being made into a dead end. These empty properties were soon to make way for the new inner relief road, as did the Queen's Hotel which closed in 1977. The wooden building (foreground) housed the shoe repairing business of Mr. H. Adey for many years, and the wall on the left guards the cutting of the LNER loop line, last used in the 1960's.

The British School of Industry, Hollis Lane. Built in 1843, it operated as a private school for up to 200 boys (paying 2d. to 6d. a week) for forty years, after which the pupils used the new Hipper Street premises. Further short periods of school use ensued, followed by various existences as a spiritual meeting house, dance hall, and food warehouse before demolition in the 1970's.

The Parish Church of St. Mary and All Saints, c. 1900. Erected on the site of an earlier church, it is over 750 years old and is the largest in Derbyshire, being 173ft. long and 110ft. wide. The wooden, lead-clad spire, just resting on the tower surface, rises 228ft. over the town and weighs an estimated 98 tons.

St. Mary's Gate in about 1890. Church Lane may just be seen on the left, with Spa Lane on the right. Inns proliferated on this ancient thoroughfare and the Plough may be seen opposite Church Lane and the Hare and Greyhound just south of the church, where it was rebuilt in 1924.

Spa Lane from Church Lane, c. 1900. The Plough Inn has gone and the cottages seen on the north side went soon after, but the house on the corner of Station Road survived to the 1960's.

Church Lane in the late 1920's. The new Crooked Spire public house was built for the Brampton Brewery on the site of these cottages in 1931.

Church Alley was pulled down in the late 1920's and early 1930's. It comprised two rows of terraced cottages at right angles to Church Lane, four on the town side of the alley and six on the east side. Behind the workmen studying form can be seen the vicarage, which survived until the 1990's.

Another aspect of Church Alley in the 1920's. The more distant of the two groups is standing by the access to the old Crooked Spire Inn yard and the rear of houses and cottages on St. Mary's Gate.

Spa Lane, c. late 1950's. After removal of cottages to build the new Employment Exchange in the 1930's (on left of frame) these houses were usefully employed to the middle of the 1950's, as were the much older ones around them.

Spa Lane-Station Road, c. 1958. Behind these houses were communal yards serving up to fifteen dwellings, the fashion in the 1800's, which could be found the length of St. Mary's Gate and Lordsmill Street. Set into the kerb on the steep Spa Lane can be seen iron scotches against which to rest waggon wheels and assist the brakes, if any.

Station Road in 1951. This road was known as Bishop's Mill Lane (the mill being near Crow Lane) prior to the coming of the railways and station. Apart from the white *Derbyshire Times* offices on the left and the shadowed gates of Shentall's Vegetable Wholesalers on the right, all these homes have been wiped out since the photograph was taken – a whole community if Mill Street and Eyre Street to the east are included.

St. Mary's Gate in the 1920's. All the buildings in the photograph have now gone, with the exception of the White Swan Hotel. Mellors' confectionery shop survived the war and the quaint Crooked Spire restaurant next door thrived as a chip shop during the war years and after. The buildings south of the Swan were demolished to Spa Lane to create the present car park and offices.

A curious triangular block on Corporation Street. Largely empty in 1977 when pictured, only the small book shop survived on the trade of passing railway customers till demolition for the relief road in 1983. The thick end of the wedge had prospered as Freeman's Temperance Hotel in pre-war years.

Stephenson Memorial Hall, c. 1900. Opened by the Duke of Devonshire in July 1879, nearly forty years after George Stephenson's death, the Hall was designed in the neo-Gothic style by the Manchester architects Smith & Woodhouse. Over £8,000 was raised by public subscription towards the total expenditure of £13,700, and the complex comprised not only a public hall but also a lecture hall and many other rooms for classes in Science and Art. Also included were a reading room, public library and even a laboratory. The hall has had a chequered history of uses, including a theatre, cinema (the Corporation Theatre after purchase by the town council in 1926) and a theatre once more today – now called the Pomegranate. The west end of the building, in which the library was situated on the first floor, was used as a Council Chamber and Mayor's Parlour to 1938, when the new Town Hall was built, after which the library occupied all the west end till it in turn moved to new accommodation. It is pleasing to note that the old building is in good order and that the long-awaited Chesterfield Museum has opened its doors here, using the whole of the beautifully restored west wing.

Stephenson Place in about 1905. At that time it was part of Knifesmithgate, which extended from Holywell Street to Packer's Row. Wardell's confectionery business, which had a retail outlet opposite and, later, on Knifesmithgate, had moved their works to Park Road, and all the property shown was soon to be removed.

The Picture House, as it was known until the Oscar Deutsch Co. acquired it in 1936 and, in 1938, changed its name to the Odeon. It first showed silent films in September 1923 (Buster Keaton in *The Playhouse*) and talking movies from 1930 (Jack Buchanan in *Paris*). One of the pianists in the silent film days was Reginald Dixon of Blackpool Tower fame, who possibly learned to play the organ here. The last film shown was *Escape from New York* with Kent Russell in October 1981. Following purchase by the Corporation, it was later opened as The Winding Wheel.

Holywell Street corner in the 1890's. This atmospheric study of the church and the stone-roofed buildings was taken from a high floor on the north side of Holywell Street. Redfern the butcher was long established in the town and the building to the right was once the Cross Keys Inn.

Durrant Road in 1983, at its junction with Tapton Lane and Felkin Street. All these properties are now gone, mainly to make way for the inner relief road. Eyres' Cabinet Works can be seen on the left and the old Hide and Skin Company premises beyond.

Infirmary Road, late 1970's. Only the foundations of the old wooden station, built in 1893 when the Manchester, Sheffield and Lincolnshire Railway Co. opened the line to Sheffield, survive. The large building of the College of Technology dates from the 1960's and the smaller block to the right from the 1920's.

Hurst House, c. 1920. Built in 1847 on land bought from the Duke of Devonshire, Hurst House was occupied by two doctors, S. Worthington in 1902 and Albert Green, who purchased it for £1,300 and sold it in 1928 to the Grammar School opposite. Initially used as the Headmaster's house, it became the Junior School (forms 1, 2 and Remove) in 1934. When the school moved to Brookside in 1964 it became a full-time Adult Education Centre.

The Rendezvous Ballroom (c. 1928) was in use as a Palais de Dance from 1925-30, having had a history as a warehouse for Wm. & Saml. Burkitt Bros., Maltsters. Between 1930 and 1939 it staged boxing matches, and after its cellars had been used as air-raid shelters became a roller-skating rink, latterly reverting to warehouse storage for Stylax Mattresses.

The Sheffield Road at Stonegravels, c. 1910, with tram tracks and overheads in evidence. What was left of the cobbled road outside of the rails did not permit much other traffic when a tram was under way!

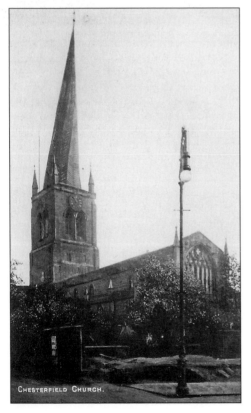

CHESTERFIELD CHURCH.

St. Mary's from the north-east, c. 1907. A rare view of the church showing the aspect not seen since the Stephenson Place frontage of Furness Chambers was erected just after this date by Thos. Furness, a local chemist and dentist. In the days when it was not common to own a watch, or even a clock, the west clock face of the church was usefully illuminated by gas jets.

Saltergate in the 1920's. All the property to the left disappeared in the 1970's to become a fine car park! The Shakespeare Inn, a Brampton Brewery house, sold its last pint in 1973, and the Turf Tavern on Holywell Street closed in 1930, but not before its successor, the Punch Bowl, the inheritor of its licence, was built behind it. The Volunteer Inn can just be seen alongside, with the Bluebell opposite, and other public houses the other side of the block; this area was well-served with drinking places! Saltergate was almost certainly named after the route along which pack-horse trains in medieval times brought rock salt to the town from Northwich in Cheshire. It remains a busy commuter road to this day.

Almshouses, Saltergate, about 1900. Eleven three-roomed dwellings were built in 1875, using bequests from Thomas Large, Sarah Rose and Geo. Taylor for what was laid down as 'poor persons of good character'. New almshouses were provided on St. Helen's Close for the modern occupiers in 1971, when the demolition of these well-liked homes created still more space for parked cars.

Saltergate in 1982, just after demolition of the old properties on Broad Pavement corner lately occupied by Staffordshire Farmers. The north side houses Evans Glass, barber Graham More, and the Red Cross.

Saltergate in the 1930's. The three-storied houses were removed in that decade, but the war intervened and redevelopment was delayed until the 1970's. The space left housed a static water tank – emergency supply for fire-fighting – and was also used as a bus park. The passage is labelled 'Court No. 1' and led to a small open area at the rear of the Unitarian Chapel.

Shepley's Yard in the early 1900's. Running south from Saltergate, this was typical of Chesterfield's many yards, most of them occupied by small cottages built for the local working class. This yard joined Saltergate to Knifesmithgate and may owe its name to Geo. Shepley, a plumber and glazier in Knifesmithgate who was elected a councillor in 1835.

Elder Way from Saltergate, c. 1920. The name probably derives from Ellar Yard, meaning 'elder tree enclosure', a narrow passageway to the north-west end of Knifesmithgate before the wholesale demolition and widening in the late '20's. Between the two roads stands the Elder Yard Chapel – now the Unitarian Chapel – suggesting that the Yard was there before the chapel was built in 1694.

Elder Way in 1934, after widening and some obvious refurbishment two years earlier. Already the Corporation had defrayed some of the improvement expenses by selling 2,124 square yards of land to the Co-operative Society for £8,444 and also 294 square yards to the Trustees of the Elder Yard Chapel to form the present forecourt.

Four old houses on the new Elder Way were removed in the 1930's for office redevelopment, leaving the west end of the Unitarian Chapel in full view. The chapel was founded in 1694 by Cornelius Clarke as a place of worship for 'dissenting Protestants' and was used mainly by Presbyterians, with Independent worshippers later allowed use at other times until 1721. The title 'Unitarian' seems to have been adopted about 1818.

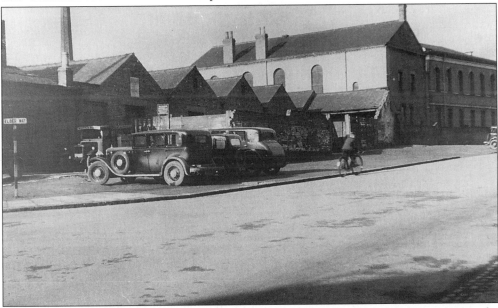

The western edge of Elder Way about 1934. Having bought the land from the Corporation, the Co-operative Society erected their fine new store where these cars are parked and extending to the edge of this photograph, where stood the entrance to a large two-storey Assembly Hall. (The second phase of what is now called 'The Department Store' was completed to Saltergate in 1959.) The building to the right is the concert hall and schoolrooms of the Methodist Church.

Saltergate in 1934, with old cottages being demolished opposite Elder Way. They were removed as far as A. W. Cooke's plumber's store, which survived until well after the war. The passage entrance is labelled 'Court No. 2' and merely led to a small yard, although there was possibly a score of houses behind this front, reached via an opening below Cooke's shop.

Wesleyan Chapel, Saltergate, c. 1910. John Wesley preached in the town in 1776 and again in the Market Place the following year. He is reported to have been well received. A Methodist Society was formed, meeting initially in Moore's Yard off Packer's Row. This chapel was built in 1795, with extensions in 1822.

Knifesmithgate in 1900 extended round to Holywell Street, the only outlet at the west end being Packer's Row and the footpath which is now Elder Way. The street thus joined the old market, just north of the church, with the new, existing, market. The word 'gate', common in the town, means 'street', but the preceding part of the name is now thought to come not directly from an old trade but from a family name, Knyfsmith or Knyfsmythe, mentioned in 14th century documents.

The Friends' Meeting House, Saltergate, about 1950. George Fox, the founder of this movement, was imprisoned at Derby and at Chesterfield, but it was at Derby that he and his adherents were first called Quakers by a Justice. Various meeting places are recorded for the young religion in the area – houses near Ashover and near Boythorpe and Tupton – but it was not until 1697 that a permanent place of worship was established in Saltergate opposite the Wesleyan Chapel. The building was a simple structure with the customary Quaker gallery and cost £70. It was demolished when the space was required for a multi-storey car park in the 1970's. Among Quakers married there were Mary Storrs and John Fry, whose son Joseph founded the famous chocolate company. The Society of Friends now meets in new premises on Goldwell Hill.

Knifesmithgate at about the turn of the century, showing how the street curved to Holywell Street, there being no through traffic to High Street. On the far left can be seen a passage to Shepley's Yard (a walk-way still existing although all the property on the north side disappeared in the 1920's to make way for the colonnade popularly known as the 'Vic Arches'.

The junction of Cavendish Street and Knifesmithgate in the early '30's. A Corporation trolley-bus inspector stands near the terminus of several routes between properties due for demolition. Tinleys shoe shop would soon be rebuilt and the block to the right demolished as far as Broad Pavement and replaced by the Regal Cinema and associated shops in 1936.

Broad Pavement in the 1920's. This old photograph brings out the ancient, almost medieval, character of this town centre way, once the only connection between two of the oldest streets, Saltergate and Knifesmithgate. In antiquity it was known as Narrow Lane. All the buildings shown are now gone save those at the end, currently (1994) being renovated.

The Knifesmithgate entrance to Broad Pavement in about 1935. Property on the corner of Cavendish Street has gone and the pavements have been lined up with the new mock-Tudor development to the west. Then, as now, cars were parked as soon as space became available.

Shepley's Yard in the 1970's. Temporary shops (Portakabins) stood here for some months until new premises were built elsewhere in town. The new lower Saltergate development is not quite under way and some of the old property in Broad Pavement still stands. The Regal Cinema towers in the background.

The last building remaining on the old section of Broad Pavement waits forlornly for the bull-dozer in the early 1980's. The Royal Hospital, seen beyond across the huge new car park, was under notice, its successor already under construction at Calow.

Another small house, c. 1961. This tiny dwelling was to be found in what many townspeople knew as Hitchcock's Yard on Knifesmithgate. Fortunately, many of the old buildings on the south side of this street have been preserved, often, as on High Street, having just their shop fronts kept up to date. Mr. Hitchcock ran the chemist's shop opposite the Victoria cinema for many years.

The end of Knifesmithgate in the early 1920's. On the left may be seen the entrance to Elder Way, then a footpath to Saltergate. The shop being dismantled was, apparently, Booker's café, which moved to Burlington Street. Their new premises were later removed for the Marks & Spencer extension in the 1930's.

Knifesmithgate in the early 1930's, before the centre shops in Glumangate were removed to create access to Rose Hill and the Town Hall site. The popular 'King and Miller', originally a Chesterfield Brewery pub, was closed in 1967 and removed to make way for Littlewood's store. Service Motors, opposite, was taken over by the Co-op and is now their D.I.Y. store and travel agency.

Cavendish Street corner in the early 1930's. Shops were removed before Cavendish House was built for new shops and first floor offices. Then, as now, any vacant lot became a car park, and blank walls were used for fly-posting. The notices on the wall refer to a 'Novel about Chesterfield' in the *Daily Dispatch*, the widening of Horns Bridge and a free gift with *Mab's Weekly*.

Cavendish Street in 1905. The no. 8 tram, en route to Whittington, has stopped where motor buses still pick up passengers. To judge from the umbrella shading a person on the top deck, the shadows and the boater, it would appear to be a fine summer's day. The large store, City House, selling drapery, mantles, ulsters, costumes, gents' and mourning clothing, was owned by McLanachan & Son. At this time it was running a closing-down sale prior to demolition and its replacement by Williams Deacon Bank, now the Royal Bank of Scotland, in the following year.

The same street in the early 1930's, just before all the buildings on the left were removed to build the Regal Cinema. The bank opposite is well established and most of the shops adjacent have been refurbished. The fly posters now advertise T. Greaves 'easy terms' – £20 worth of goods for 4/6d. (22½p.) per week. At the far end of the street, the Turf Tavern on Holywell Street is being dismantled to reveal its replacement, the Punch Bowl, already standing behind it.

Saltergate-Cavendish Street corner in the late 1930's. Following the pattern mentioned above, the Mansfield Brewery operated the Blue Bell Inn whilst the new one was being erected behind it. Shops and offices were also included in the development, while to the left the new Regal Cinema had opened its doors in October 1936 with the Astaire and Rogers film *Follow the Fleet!*

Stephenson Place in about 1930. The popular Arcade, which afforded a short cut to Cavendish Street, was trading, and Wardell's sweet shop, opposite their factory and bakery for many years, is being dismantled. They later retailed from a shop in Knifesmithgate up until the post-war years. The Lord Nelson pub was also refurbished about this time, in the then-fashionable mock-Tudor style.

Holywell Street in the mid-30's, but before 1938 as evidenced by the trolley bus overheads. The street widening following the disappearance of the Turf Tavern is nearly completed. The building in the centre, known as Damm's Corner after the fruit shop there for many years, divides the traffic between Saltergate and Holywell Cross. Next to it was Watts, the well-known tripe shop and, beyond, the Shakespeare Inn.

Holywell Street, c. 1934. The Turf Tavern is roofless and the apex of its successor, the Punch Bowl, can just be seen above the shop next door. This hairdressing business moved to Cavendish Street nearby, before demolition for road improvements. The Volunteer Inn was operated by Smith's Brewery up to 1940, and the Hygienic Bakery by Geo. Hoare to the 1960's or 1970's.

The Livingstone Café & Coffee House in the early 1880's. This popular café on the corner of Packer's Row and Burlington Street operated for many years until Swallows took over the premises, redeveloping the end of the block in 1930 and trading from there until 1970. At the time of the photograph Swallows' shop was next door with a bee-hive over the door.

High Street in the 1890's. This charming old photograph portrays many aspects of life at that time: the popularity of headwear, gas lighting, horse drays and handcarts and the outside displays of goods. The offices of the *Derbyshire Courier* may be seen on the site now used by Marks & Spencer. This was the forerunner of the present *Derbyshire Times*, having been previously known as the *Chesterfield Gazette*. Their printing at this time was done in Dealing Yard, later used as Woodhead's warehouse.

High Street in 1905, with the no. 8 tram on its way westward. At this time Burlington Street was so narrow at the east end that trams were not permitted to pass through on busy market days, the Brampton and Whittington parts having their own termini on Low Pavement and Stephenson Place respectively. The presence of no. 8 in this position thus denotes a non-market day. The street is busy, nevertheless, being crowded with handcarts and cabs. Boots began trading in the town in 1895, gradually acquiring property until their store occupied the whole block, with the exception of the arched Cathedral Vaults. Taylor Bros. bought the drapery business of Hewitt & Heane in 1887 and specialised in mourning clothing, while Seaman & Sons' photographic studios opposite had established a thriving business in the district.

High Street, looking west, in about 1900. A summer morning, judging by the shadows, with much evidence of horse traffic on the road. Woodhead's, first established opposite as a tea and coffee importer in 1829 by James Woodhead of Liverpool, opened the head stores on High Street in 1898 with a warehouse in Dealing Yard on the other side of Packer's Row. They traded all round the area, with branch shops as far apart as Bakewell and Poolsbrook.

High Street in 1903. This photograph, taken from T. P. Wood's offices above the archway over the pavement, first appeared in Wood's well-known Almanac. This was evidently a market day, judging by the varied collection of horse vehicles.

A summer scene in the Market Place in about 1903. It is late evening but the the sun is still hot to judge from the parasol. Two little girls are decked out in white frocks and black boots, while others stand under the arches of the Cathedral Vaults, known locally, from the stained glass, as the Pretty Windows. The car is thought to be an early Renault.

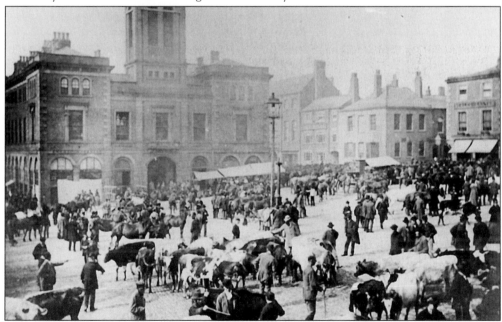

Market Square, 1882. September Fair day and the cattle market in the main square. It seems that horses had pride of place in the centre and cattle were in the Low Pavement area in those horse power days. The corniced building used to be the Town Hall, and opposite is the Westminster Bank which was superseded a few years later in 1904 (its successor has in turn been replaced). The old Star Inn is between the bank and the Angel Hotel.

Another view of High Street in 1903 from the T.P. Wood's office. This also appeared in his Almanac with the caption 'Looking out of my office window to the east, shewing where the trams are going.' This referred to the forthcoming advent of electric trams to replace the horse-drawn ones which plied between Low Pavement and Brampton, although they would not be in use until December 1907. There are at least nine horse-powered vehicles to be seen in the picture and, to demonstrate the fashion of the period, it is not possible to find any person without some form of headgear!

Burlington Street, c. 1900. The house standing at the end belonged to a Dr. Green and was removed in 1908, the short-lived Alpine Gardens taking its place prior to a road being laid to Lordsmill Street in 1932. Virtually all the shops on the left survive, with only the right (south) side being redeveloped. The beehive sign opposite J.K. Swallow's first shop in the town, in 1862, denotes a drapery business run by Peter Murphy and his sons up to the 1920's.

The Market Square in about 1893. The 36-year old Market Hall on the left and the stalls below the new Westminster Bank currently under construction look much as they do today. Scales & Salter, later Scales & Sons, sold footwear on the site of a previous Town Hall donated by the Duke of Rutland in 1788. It was replaced in 1913 by the Sheffield & Hallamshire, later the Midland, Bank.

High Street, c. 1902, dominated by the relatively new building of the Westminster Bank and the Angel Hotel to the left. The shop front with awning seems to have been the main entrance on High Street. The Angel was probably the premier social centre for the town, being the venue for important functions and banquets. In addition it received coaches and had stabling in a yard that extended to Saltergate. The hotel closed in 1915 and, following a disastrous fire in 1917, it was demolished in 1926 for bank expansion.

The corner of Market Place in the early 1900's. This shop was retailing drugs long before Joseph Bettison built up the business from 1804. He was partnered by Booth until 1885, when their assistants, Sampson and Barfoot, bought the shop. F. W. Dutton took over the ownership in 1926, continuing until the early 1950's. It later became Wakefield's Army Stores and then an Abbey National Bank branch in 1993.

Central Pavement in about 1930. Turner Bros. on the left had been in the town as drapers and clothiers since the 1840's and were soon to build the mock-Tudor-faced store on Packer's Row and Vicar Lane to the right of the frame, the frontage of which has been preserved. The Yorkshire Penny Bank, dating from 1899, shows a corner entrance long since sealed off.

Church Lane in 1952. Wakefield's Army Stores then occupied the small shop on the corner of Packer's Row and the Shambles currently used by Thorntons. Brights Gents' Outfitters were on the other corner. The building on the left is the Settlement, an organisation founded mainly by Miss Violet Markham, sister of C. P. Markham and a town councillor, to foster voluntary educative work among mothers with young children. The wall on the right concealed Woodhead's warehouse and bakery.

The Royal Oak, Middle Shambles, in the 1880's. Said to be one of the oldest public houses in the town, this may originally have been two butcher's shops in this meat-handling area. It was not licensed as an inn until 1772. The corner of one of the many over-hanging roofs can be seen on the right, above the gossiping ladies in their tarred hats and shawl.

Tontine Road and Central Pavement in the early 1930's. Frederick Barker's Milliners and Drapery shop stood on this site from the 1800's, before Tontine Road was constructed in around 1914 following the razing of the Dog Kennels and the removal of the Three Tuns public house.

The same site in the late 1970's. Barkers redeveloped the property in 1937 and traded until the late 1950's. The police station extension, including garages, occupies Tontine Road to New Beetwell Street. This site now forms part of the McDonald fast food chain.

New Beetwell Street and Tontine Road prior to development in the 1920's. The Borough police station was in the house next to the fire appliance and ambulance garage. The fire service used the old Theatre Yard behind for hose drill and drying.

The new police headquarters in the 1930's. The centre building was divided into two flats housing the Police Fire Brigade Superintendent Hawksworth and Police Inspector Hogg. The smaller house, adjacent to Falcon Yard, was used as a Charge Office by the police force.

58

Further police station improvements took place in 1937, with the removal of the old house and an eastward extension of the new building. The opening ceremony was performed by H.M. Inspector of Constabulary Lt. Col. F. Brook.

New Beetwell Street in the 1950's. The demolition of part of Legard's Leather Stores takes place for road improvements. The old 1849 Court House is still in use ahead of the new one opening on West Bars in 1965. Legard's finally closed in the 1970's.

Lower Tontine Road in the 1940's. The site used by the East Midland bus service was occupied during the war by the Auxiliary Fire Service as a headquarters and, it seems, for drying hoses.

This large building photographed in around 1950 stood adjacent to the old workhouse which was built in 1763, just south of the existing bowling green, and was the home of the Workhouse Master. The houses on the left, bordering the green, were used for the accommodation of police and fire personnel. The ground on which cars are parked was once part of Ward's Yard.

Packers' Row in the early 1900's. John Turner, the wholesale and retail drapers, occupied two premises at 5 and 9 Packers' Row, and was soon to develop the site as it now stands. They were established in 1845 and traded until taken over in the 1980's. The Commercial Hotel, owned then by the Tadcaster Brewery Co., boasted twelve bedrooms and two dining rooms. Geo. Edge, the printer, eventually moved to West Bars.

The Clothing Hall was on the corner of Packers' Row in 1890. The cast-iron gas lamp was first erected on the south-east corner of the Market Place in 1824 and was lit by gas produced by Joseph Bower, a tinsmith, in a cellar adjacent to the Cathedral Vaults. In 1970 the lamp was refurbished and, now electrified, casts its light in St. Mary's churchyard.

Central Pavement in the 1970's, with flared trousers now in fashion. A 'No Entry' sign has replaced the old gas lamp and much of this area stands ready for development. The 'Panda Car' is emerging from Theatre Yard, at the south end of which was the police headquarters.

Low Pavement, c. 1975. Shops have been vacated for the once-controversial, but finally successful, Pavements scheme. Greaves chemist's moved to Vicar Lane, but other businesses, like Kirks and Colleges, closed their doors permanently. The famous tax-dodging long window, on the Tontine Road side of Greaves, has been removed for safe-keeping.

The Peacock Inn in 1974, with a temporary roof covering fire damage from earlier in the year. This providential fire revealed ancient oak frames, which indicated a building of considerable historic importance dating from the Middle Ages. It is now restored and preserved as a heritage and exhibition centre.

For many years this elegant house stood in South Place between the old Slipper Baths and Messrs. Yeomans' Saddlery. It was latterly the home of Thomas Dodd, a dealer in scrap at Brampton.

South Street, c. 1900, a busy place at that time with a microcosm of the town's trade able to exist on the custom afforded by so much housing in the nearby Dog Kennels. Almost all necessary suppliers were here, from barbers to confectioners, butchers to watchmakers, not to mention the two public houses, the Commercial Hotel and the Bricklayers' Arms. Some of these properties have been carefully restored and survive to the present day.

South Street and Beetwell Street in the 1950's. This once-elegant corner building housed a thriving radio business ('black flex one penny a yard') but it closed in the wartime years and a few transitory retailers used the premises. In 1958, just before demolition, Abbots sold horse-meat and pet food from the lower part. Mr. Marriott's cycle shop survived here and on Lordsmill Street into the 1990's.

Beetwell Street, c. 1880. On this old print a larger Tudor hall can be seen in the position occupied by Yeomans Stores since 1887. This is Beetwell Hall and the street may derive its name from it or, possibly, from the Chesterfield Bete family of mediaeval times. It was demolished in the early 1880's after being used as a warehouse for a nearby shop.

Beetwell Street in 1958, hardly recognisable as the much wider thoroughfare of today: all the property in sight has gone, demolished either for car-parking space or for the new Police Station.

Lordsmill Street and Beetwell Street, c. 1934. Several dwellings have already been removed for redevelopment, and the multi-storey houses on the north side were to go soon after but a little matter of the Second World War intervened. Through the opening under the mock-Tudor building on the A61 can just be seen Bath Place, where the 'smallest house' (page 15) was sited.

Beetwell Street in 1958, this time looking west. In 1918 the J. Green undertaking establishment building had housed a club, but Green's later traded here for many years before being succeeded by Kennings Specialised Services. The new police headquarters was erected on this site in the 1970's.

Demolition well under way on Beetwell Street in the 1950's – the once-elegant shops and dwellings are being flattened, initially to accommodate temporary cabin shops and later for municipal car parks. Ellse, one of the last of the once-numerous pawnbrokers, had traded since before 1912.

A Court House detail photographed just prior to removal in the 1960's. The Municipal Hall was built in 1849 by Sam Walters of Chesterfield and cost £1,270. This part was used as the Borough Petty Sessions Court until the 1960's and also as a police office to 1926, when the new police station was opened opposite. One wonders about the fate of these handsome stone carvings – were they reduced to hardcore or did they just vanish, like the rare firemark on a building opposite?

Wheeldon Lane (c. 1930) was once one of the main streets to the south from the Market Place. Lace factories, owned by Beardmore & Waterhouse and using child labour in the 1830's, were to be found in it as well as, later, George Mason's Tobacco Works. New Beetwell Street was brought across at about this point in the 1920's, necessitating flights of steps to negotiate it and follow the lane down to the exit by the Ragged School.

The Dog Kennels, c. 1900, the popular name for the area to the west of the bowling green extending down to the River Hipper and, according to contemporary commentator, Pendleton, 'the scene of riot and wild debauchery'. This part of Chesterfield consisted of some 200 crowded old properties housing up to 600 residents, mainly Irishmen working on the railways or at Staveley Works and using workmen's train (the 'Paddy Mail') to get there.

Bradshaw Place, c. 1900, another part of the Dog Kennel area. Removal of this over-crowded and insanitary area became the personal crusade of Mayor Charles P. Markham, who spent his own money, estimated to be £10,000, clearing the centuries-old properties and constructing a new road from South Place to the Queen's Park Road. This was done by 1912 and the new thoroughfare was named after Markham by a grateful Corporation.

Soresby Street in the 1930's. A school was built here in 1815 to cater for 300 pupils. Managed by the Anglican National Society, it was linked to the Church of St. Mary, later Holy Trinity. In 1903 the attendance was reported as 419 children and, in spite of proposals to rebuild, the school was closed in 1930. The small corner shop was last used by Wheatcroft, General Dealer and Tobacconist.

Glumangate corner of Saltergate in about 1920. Nothing to do with glue, this unique street name is now thought to be derived from 'Glenmanestrete', mentioned in 13th century papers and meaning 'Street of the Minstrels', although the reason is unclear. The ale-house on Saltergate selling Bass was the Miners Arms, previously known as the Fountain Inn.

Glumangate in the 1920's. Irving's Corn Merchants used much of the road below the future Rose Hill and, like the Queen's Head public house on the left, were later to redevelop in the Chesterian mock-Tudor-with-colonnades style.

The Westminster Bank decorated, probably, for the coronation of Edward VII. To be seen in this photograph are the stone cobbled streets with the tramlines newly laid and the overhead cables. A milk float with churns seems to be delivering to the Angel, then the largest hotel in the town centre; it would close in 1915.

The Star and Garter, c. 1935. Standing at the west edge of New Square, or Swines Green as it was known when sheep and pigs were sold there, this pub was owned by Scarsdale Brewery, who closed it in 1937, transferring its licence to their new house, the Walton Hotel.

Star and Garter yard. The inn was residential in its heyday, and had ample stabling in the yard behind, with access from New Square and also from West Bars. The block was redeveloped in the 1950's, along with Dent's new shop.

Schofield's Yard in the early 1930's. This yard, with perhaps a dozen terrace houses, ran north of New Square with access past the east side of Dr. Stoke's house, now the Yorkshire Bank.

West Bars in the 1920's, showing shops that will be well remembered by many: Dents on the corner of New Square, the newsagent's shop later kept by Troths, Urtons the Ironmonger's, Walkers the Saddler's, and Rider the Watchmaker. The tram tracks are clearly seen, as is the entrance to the Star and Garter Yard by the row of buckets.

West Bars in 1885. The decorations outside the old Sun Inn are in honour of the mayor for the coming year, Alderman T.P. Wood. This photograph shows the wooden building which still stands, albeit much altered, in use as a hairdressing salon. The basket-making business of W. Nadin is just beyond. Thomas Philpott Wood, 1840-1911, was one of Chesterfield's greatest benefactors: an Alderman of the town, he ran a successful wine and spirit business on High Street, in the Market Place, and lived at Brambling House at Hady. With E.J. Maynard he was the first elected member for Chesterfield for the County Council and was Mayor of the Borough in 1873, 1885 and 1886. He was instrumental in constructing the Queen's Park for the town, not only donating £500 but raising other monies towards it, and was accorded the honour of opening the park in 1887 to mark the Queen's Jubilee. When the Park Annexe was purchased as a memorial to the Queen in 1901, he gave another £500 towards its cost; he also gave Alpine Gardens to the town as well as the park bandstand and the Mayoral Chain of Office. He was made the second Honorary Freeman of the Borough in 1887.

Rose Hill (c. 1930) stood on the site of the present Town Hall and was possibly the first brick-built house in the town, in 1730. Erected by a family called Thornhill, it passed through several ownerships, notably that of John Brown, a local Alderman who was agent to the Hunloke family, and the Butchers of Cutthorpe Hall, before removal in 1936.

West Bars in about 1912. A special tramcar, no. 15, carrying 2,000 gallons of water, sprays the roads around its tracks. The necessity for this is not far away in the picture: horses, drays and carts all in evidence! On the right is the LDEC rail station, and on the left is the entrance to the Park Hotel, the then business of the old West House.

West Row, West Bars, c. 1950, an externally attractive terrace of stone-faced dwellings on the south side of West Bars. Built in the 1800's near Maynards Meadow, also known as Maynard's Row, these twenty-four dwellings were removed in the 1960's for the construction of a multi-storey car park.

West Row, the brick-built rear of the row, leading to the curve of Boythorpe Road. This photograph shows the outside toilets and coal storage between the houses and gardens.

Clarence Road in the early 1900's. Photography was still a rare sight at the start of the century and there were often several people attracted by the photographer's preparations, even for simple record shots such as were taken for postcard purposes. The groups invariably add interest to the picture.

West Bars in about 1910. Traders in this area supplied most of the essentials for local residents, including as they did a baker, grocer, butcher and chemist. The Chesterfield Co-operative Society occupied (and still does) the premises on the right, on the corner of Rutland Road. This was the district headquarters for five other branches in outlying areas.

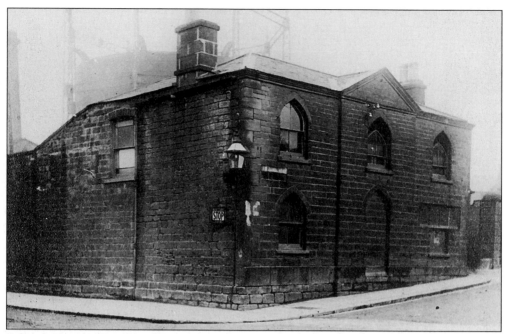

Foljambe Road, 1910. The original offices of the Chesterfield Gas and Water Co. were built when the gasworks was brought into production in 1826, at the bottom of Foljambe Road, previously known as Pothouse Lane. Gas charges were calculated according to the number of burners supplied to the premises at about 12/6d. (or $62\frac{1}{2}$p) per 1,000 cu.ft. Apparently, a dry gasholder was in use at that time and is nearly full of gas. These offices were replaced in 1910 at a cost of £2,820.

These quaintly shaped houses stood near Field House, once the home of William Bradbury Robinson, on the site of the present York House and adjacent to Brewery Yard.

Holywell Street in the 1890's. The house to the right of centre was removed in the early 1930's, probably to give better access to the rear of the Shakespeare Inn, and the remainder followed in the early 1970's. The building with the inn sign next to Eyres' furniture store was the Moulders Arms. One feature in many of these old prints is the number of flagpoles on all kinds of buildings; people liked to show the flag frequently in days gone by! Masts can be seen here not only on the small shop but also on Eyres and even the Crooked Spire tower.

Holywell Street, at its junction with Newbold Road and Sheffield Road, in about 1900, with a pause for a change of horses for the loaded cart. The entrance to Holywell House, which may at that time have housed a 'Ladies School and Kindergarten' under Principals the Misses Cooper and Turner, can just be made out on the right of the frame.

The view above in the 1980's. Holywell House, on the right, was then a post-graduate Medical Training Centre. The car showroom and the filling station beyond have now disappeared and the area awaits new development.

The Devonshire Arms, Holywell Street in the 1950's. One of no less than nine licensed houses on Holywell Street at various times, this Tennants pub closed in the late 1960's, in common with the rest of the immediate area, for road improvements,

The Queen's Park, c. 1910. When T.P. Wood was offered, on being made an Honorary Freeman of the Borough in 1887, a silver casket to contain the scroll, he asked that the money subscribed be used to build a bandstand in the park he had done so much to provide. It was erected near the lake, in an area which is now a children's playground: the stand now being restored is one of three to be found in old prints.

Feeding the ducks in about 1915. Apart from the style of dress and the height of the trees, this same scene can be observed by the park lake today.

The Wheatsheaf, Newbold, in the 1960's. Built as the village school in 1785, it became a public house in 1863, keeping its licence for 100 years before removal in 1965 to facilitate road improvements. The new Wheatsheaf, erected slightly further back, was opened in February 1966.

Two

Industry

The tobacco factory in about 1900. George Mason was cutting tobacco in Wheeldon Lane in the early 1800's, moving his factory to Spital Mills in the 1860's where it became one of the largest of its kind in England. The 'Cropper' cigarettes did not become popular with the smoking public and the mill – still standing – ceased tobacco manufacture in about 1907.

The firm of Plowright Brothers was founded in 1875 and made heavy engineering equipment, chiefly for the mining industry, at their works in Brampton for several generations, exporting worldwide. This photograph shows the north end of the erecting shop.

Known as the German crane, because of its origin, this 140-ton cantilever crane was a landmark in Markham's Broad Oaks works for over fifty years. The works was acquired by Charles Paxton Markham in 1888-9 from the liquidators of Wm. Oliver & Co. and Markham built it into a heavy engineering concern pre-eminent in its field. Amongst its achievments are the construction of the Goonhilly Down radio telescope, segments for the London Underground and, more recently, boring machines for the Channel Tunnel.

Blast furnaces of the Staveley Coal & Iron Co. in 1934. Established on the site of Barrow's earlier iron working, the modern works were founded by Charles Markham and Richard Barrow in 1863, Markham being Managing Director. He married Rosa Paxton, daughter of Joseph Paxton, designer of the Crystal Palace and later knighted, and one of their five children was Charles Paxton Markham. C.P. Markham was to build up an industry so diverse in its products and so integrated in its methods of manufacture as to be almost self-sufficient – it owned coal and ironstone mines, limestone quarries and salt mines. Many of the by-products of iron making and much of the waste energy went into the production of chemicals of all kinds. Alderman Charles Paxton Markham died suddenly in 1926, leaving an indelible mark on Chesterfield's history. The Company is now fragmented, and the two businesses on the Hollingwood site – pipe making and chemicals – are both French-owned.

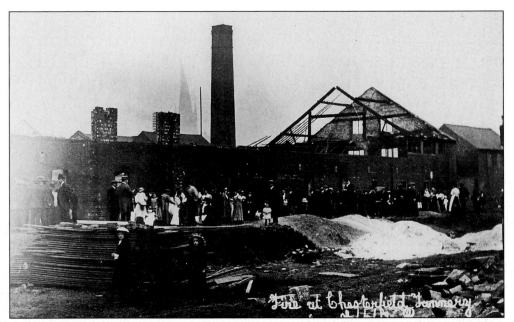

Clayton's Tannery, June 17th 1913. A photograph postcard, by A.R. Rippon, taken following the fire which destroyed the premises in 1913, despite the Midland Railway fire train coming the 24 miles from Derby in 22 minutes! The factory was rebuilt from the ashes of the 1875 one and still flourishes, exporting at least fifty per cent of its production.

Scarsdale Brewery, c. 1920. A group of workers in the yard on Spa Lane pose for the camera and don't look overjoyed at the prospect. Although brewing had taken place on the site as long ago as 1822, the Scarsdale Brewery Co. Ltd. was not floated till 1865, went bankrupt in 1878 and passed through several hands, notably the Birkin family, before being taken over by Whitbread's, finally closing in 1960. The Company owned thirty-three pubs at takeover. Their most popular products were P.A. bitter and XXXX ale.

Three ages of fire appliances: the Chesterfield Fire Brigade showing their old and new appliances in 1911. The older, manual one looks to have been a museum piece even then; the 1901 engine had a steam-driven pump which delivered 350 gall per minute and was kept in Theatre Yard. The motor-driven Merryweather, with the lovely number, could not only get there quicker, but could then pump 450 galls per minute! In 1854 the four part-time firemen were paid £2 per quarter. In 1909 fifteen of the Police Force of thirty-five acted as firemen; even up to the early 1930's the Chief Constable of the Borough also acted as Captain of the Fire Brigade, which was part of the constabulary, although by this time the brigade strength had risen to seventeen firemen and two engineers. The fire station, seen adjoining the old Court House, had to be enlarged to accommodate the new arrival, R1234. Following its demolition, to form part of New Beetwell Street, five appliances, with ambulances, were kept in the large-doored building next to the new Police Station.

Pearson's pottery, c. 1900. In this posed photograph the girls are putting the final touches to salt-glazed flagons before dispatch. As any local gardener knows, there is an abundance of clay in the area and this, allied to the nearby coal, led to many potteries being established, especially in Brampton, Newbold and Whittington. The clay was found to be best suited to brownware pottery and stoneware, kitchen pots, jugs, bottles, dishes and jars. The proximity of the railways, for easy delivery, was also a factor. James Pearson & Co., at Whittington Moor (Pottery Lane), was established in 1810, and in 1909 the owner, Johnson Pearson, an Alderman of the County Council, gave evidence at an enquiry that his total workforce, including a colliery, consisted of 628 men. Pearson's has long passed from family hands and was still trading in 1994, although its closure was announced in that year.

Another operation for ladies: a machine cuts the bung threads in a salt-glazed earthenware bottle at Pearson's.

St. George's Works in 1899. Built in 1862 by T.P. Wood to produce mineral and soda water and for general storage of wines and spirits, these premises survived the extension of Knifesmithgate to Rose Hill and were acquired by the Cooperative Society, serving as their milk depot in the 1940's and now their electrical department.

Willett's sweet factory in about 1979, on the corner of Tapton Lane and Brewery Street. Willett Bros.' sweets and confectionery business was established in the 1930's and moved to new premises at Thompson Street, Whittington when this area was required for road improvements connected with Chesterfield's new inner relief road in the 1980's.

Another sweet factory in about 1960. Robertson & Woodcock established their sweet factory in the old Chesterfield Brewery building in the latter part of the 1930's. The company was founded in London early this century and amalgamated to become Trebor-Sharpe before becoming part of the Bassett group in the 1980's. The site was bought from Kennings, who discarded the idea of a service station there, building it over the road instead.

Three

People

Although it has not been possible to identify these two gentlemen, their photographs, dating from the early 1900's, are typical of the carte de visite, popular during the period. Old photographs seldom show smiling faces – the exposures required were too long for that. These prints were made by Wm. Leuchars, Market Place, and Seaman on High Street respectively. William Leuchars, thought to be a Scot, was a fine photographer operating in the 1895-1922 period from 13 Market Place.

The Rev. Edmund Francis Crosse, Vicar of Chesterfield from 1905 and Archdeacon from 1910 to 1918. Contemporary opinion has him as a 'dynamic personality and a born organiser' and 'lovable and kind' He organised the Church of England Men's Society in the town and a boys' club in Elder Yard.

A group of wounded servicemen pose with staff of the Ashgate Wartime Hospital, most of whom were of the Volunteer Aid Detachment.

Could this have been the Home Guard in the First World War? The group of civilians and
military men in puttees seem to be posing near the Central Schools, and the stacked rifles
suggest an exercise or parade, or at least some drill. The definition on this old print is not good
enough to recognise the cap badges, but it is known that a unit of Lancashire Fusiliers was
housed in school halls in the town in 1915. Or is the group connected with the short-lived
'Derby Scheme', an effort to get military volunteers from Corporation employees? A fine body
of men, in any case!

This formidable football team may have been assembled for a charity match, perhaps for a local Miners' Relief fund during the 1921 strike, and it seems to be composed entirely of Staveley-born players. White-haired Ernest (Nudger) Needham was certainly a player of renown for Sheffield United and England. S. Bramall, referee, J. Russell (Glasgow), D. Griffin (Forest), J. Lack (Chesterfield), F. Bates (Barnsley), E. Wheatley (Rotherham County), J. Dykes (Belfast), C. Hay, A. Styles (the Wednesday), W. Lievesley (Derby County), E. Needham (Sheffield Utd.), G. Needham (Gillingham), H. Wright (Gillingham).

School photograph, c. 1910, and not a smiling face among the lot! Despite all efforts it has not been possible to identify this school group, but the expressions and varied clothing merited the photograph's inclusion.

The Salvation Army Band. This reunion of Salvation Army bandsmen took place in the early 1930's and the photograph was posed for on a piece of ground between Foundry Street and Shaw Street. The bandmaster was Arthur Tagg, fourth from the right in the second row, with his brother Hiram, the trombonist and a future Mayor of Chesterfield, second from the left in the back row.

Pottery children. This group was posed in the yard of Pearson's Pottery in the 1890's. All the lads are wearing clogs, as well as caps, and it may be that they were employed in heavier, dirtier work than the pinafored girls. It is quite likely that most of these children could not read or write, having left school to work, and so relied on attendance at Sunday School for rudimentary literacy.

Derby Road School, c. 1900. The pupils of Standard 1 sit for the photograph with their teachers.

A group of scouts from the 25th Chesterfield Troop, based at Saltergate Methodist Church, exhibit the pennant won at the County Rally and presented by the Chief Scout, Lord Rowallan. Front row: T. Nixon, T. Butler, J.T. Franks (Scoutmaster), R. Davies and D. Moore. Back row: R. Thompson, A. Clayton and P. Shelton (A.S.M.).

The staff of Knowles (Welshpool) Pottery, 1928. This pottery, though not originally one of the largest in the town, was founded by a Mr. Blake and later operated by his widow and Luke Knowles. After expansion by Matthew Knowles in 1835 and 1837, it was merged with the Briddon Pottery under George Shaw in 1914. Shaw had previously taken over the Walton Pottery and merged with the Welshpool to form the Barker concern (in Barker Lane). The group traded to 1957, and was noted for its stoneware and especially for water filters.

Hasland Swimming Club with the trophy won for life-saving training awards in about 1954. The club used the Markham swimming baths and were trained by Alderman Grace Corner (with trophy), who coached many members in life-saving techniques, receiving a special award from the R.L.S.S. for her services.

Detail from a photograph of the Revolution House at Old Whittington in about 1912. The photographer never seemed to be alone for long when he set up his tripod, and on this occasion these children add charming interest.

The library staff at their Christmas party in 1948, held after hours in the then children's library. Officials on the front row are: R. Cooper (Asst. Librarian), Mrs. G.R. Micklewright, Cllr. T. Bucknall, (Chairman Lib. Committee), Mrs. T. Bucknall, Ald. E. Smith (Mayor), Mrs. E. Smith, G.R. Micklewright (Librarian), Mrs. R. Clegg. Middle row: Mrs Hartley, Miss E. Lenthall, Mrs R. Cooper, Miss J. Sullivan, Miss B. Parsons, Miss Vera Hall, Miss J. Crapper, Miss M. Stone, Miss B. Parkin, Miss D. Hawkins. Back row: Miss B. Reid, Miss M. Hearnshaw, Mr J.K. Wikeley, Miss S. Renton, Miss J. Fox, Miss M. Hassall, Miss G. Ashmore, Miss J. Austin, Miss N. Hughes, Mr W.R. Thompson.

Four
Events

Floods were not uncommon in the School Board Lane area of Brampton, where the rain-swollen river Hipper turned through a sharp angle, in the 1920's. Hulley's bus to Bakewell and Youlgreave seems destined to be late, unless the driver can swing it into life!

After sampling electric lighting as part of festivities for the visit of Edward VII and his Queen in 1872, the Corporation paid £30 to Hammond & Co. in 1881 to try out electric arc lighting in the Market Place. This was successful, and arc lights and incandescent lamps (carbon filaments) were installed in selected places. This contemporary drawing shows one at the west gate of the Parish Church, enabling Chesterfield to lay claim to be the first English town to use electricity for street lights.

Coronation Day, 1910. As part of the celebrations a programme of events was arranged in the Queen's Park and was well attended. This shows the Mayor, Ald. Charles Paxton Markham, attended by Town Clerk John Middleton and Chief Constable Robert Kilpatrick.

Part of the crowd alongside the bedecked cricket pavilion at the Coronation Day celebrations – a collection of Sunday-best outfits.

Chesterfield Races, c. 1905. Though occasional race meetings were held from the late 17th century, they were only held regularly, though at differing times of the year, from the 1850's. The meetings were run over two days, latterly in October, and were patronised and supported by the Duke of Devonshire, in the form of prize money and refreshments at the Angel in Chesterfield.

Flat out to the finish – probably up Racecourse Road area or maybe the Stand Road straight. The famous jockey, Fred Archer, is said to have ridden here, and Lord Chesterfield's horses ran regularly. Official Jockey Club racing ceased in 1877 and the last informal race was run on 29th July, 1924.

The Chesterfield Swimming Sports, c. 1920. Normally taking place at Walton Dam, these events were highly regarded and well attended. Invariably, one or other of the photographers in the town would picture the crowds, later displaying the photographs for sale.

A sale at Messrs. Eyres, c. 1900. The dark building next to Eyres, in shadow, is the closed Moulders' Arms, soon to make way for the furniture store expansion, and opposite is the Leopard Inn, which closed in 1912 and became a newsagents before demolition in 1930.

A 'Walk' in 1912 down the road to the Queen's Park, where many different events finished up or just took place. This one is the Whitsuntide Demonstration of the Chesterfield and District Sunday School Union.

Another Sunday School walk, in about 1906, along the A61, Sheffield Road, Whittington Moor. This time they have the help of a uniformed band, possibly the Salvation Army.

Chesterfield from the north in the 1890's, taken from the track of the Midland Railway. The tents on Durrant Meadow are believed to be the Chesterfield Volunteers Camp, with upwards of thirty horses tethered there. To the right of the camp is the Chesterfield Brewery, with Crow Lane crossing the Rother on the left.

This postcard was just titled 'Skating on the Queen's Park Lake.' The dress of the only lady in the photograph seems to date it to about 1920.

The reins and traces indicate that there were four horses to haul this load of gentlemen (twenty-one, and two boys) from the Devonshire Hotel at Hasland in the early 1920's.

Several photographs exist of unauthorised 'coal-getting' from spoil heaps at local pits such as Boythorpe and Brockwell during the 1912 miners' strike; this shows the latter.

Titled 'In the Hands of the Law', this was surely an opportunist shot by an enterprising photographer in the early part of the century. The constable and sergeant appear to be taking an offender in the direction of the police station at the old Court House.

September Fair Day, 1882. Before the new cattle market was opened in July 1900, at a cost of £4,000, the market places were used for this purpose. This area saw horses and cattle, and New Square (then Swines Green) was the venue for the sale of sheep and pigs.

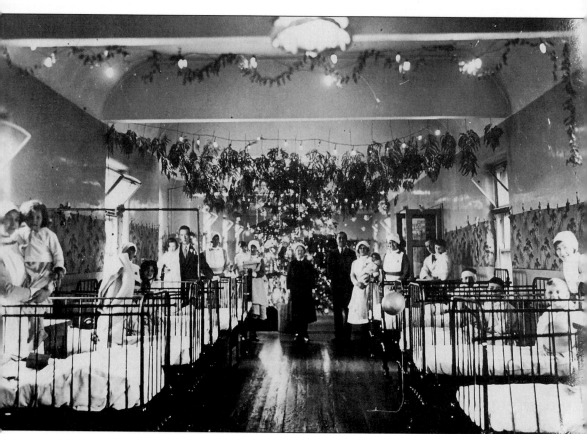

Christmas in the children's ward of the Royal Hospital in the 1910's. The first section of the Chesterfield and North Derbyshire Hospital, as it was then known, was begun in 1859, with just twelve beds. Local benefactors endowed wards over the years and the hospital expanded, with wards named after C.P. Markham, the Duke of Devonshire, Edward Eastwood, and others. Ald. Eastwood bought the Board School on Durrant Road and had it made into a medical ward, and also gave land to the north for the provision of the Nurses' Home. The hospital was reliant on voluntary contributions for its revenue, and in 1917 the businessmen of the district raised £8,000 to pay the hospital's debts, in recognition of which the King gave permission for it to be titled 'Royal Hospital'.

Aeroplane at Chesterfield, probably piloted by L.G. Hall of Sheffield, who gave demonstrations at Brookside fields in 1913. It is possible that he was sponsored by a newspaper of the time.

Earlier, in July 1912, the first recorded local flight by a heavier-than-air machine had taken place at Brampton, when B.C. Hucks landed his Bleriot aircraft in a field opposite the Terminus Hotel after a flight from Mansfield. This picture was taken on his pre-flight inspection of the landing ground.

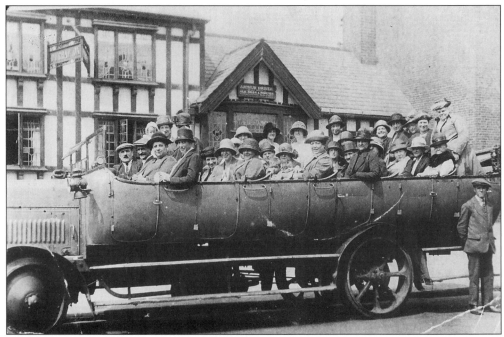

Ready for the trip. The ladies of what is thought to be the Brampton Church Sisterhood are installed in their charabanc outside the Durham Ox on Chatsworth Road. The coach may have been operated by Watkinson & Able. The make is unknown, but the oil lamps and solid tyres date it to the early 1920's. Arthur Driver kept the Durham Ox for more than thirty-two years.

In the latter part of the First World War a Tank Week was held in the town to promote Victory Loan Bonds, and these weapons were transported by the GC Railway and displayed in the Queen's Park. Two field guns, possibly these, were still on permanent display outside Ashgate Drill Hall in the 1930's.

High Street in the summer of 1904. Workmen laying the tram tracks are photographed with, as usual, plenty of onlookers. On the left may be seen the arches of T.P. Wood's offices, Hadfield's Pork Butchers, Warner's Fish Shop and the two photographers' studios, Leuchars (behind the group of men) and Seaman (opposite Taylors).

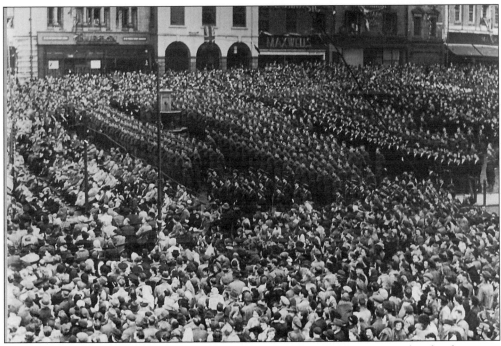

At the end of the Second World War a Day of National Prayer was announced and is the reason for this gathering in the Market Place. All services were represented and, with other local organisations, they paraded there from the Town Hall area.

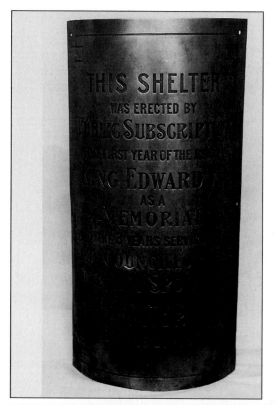

THIS SHELTER
WAS ERECTED BY
PUBLIC SUBSCRIPT
FIRST YEAR OF THE
KING EDWARD
AS A
MEMORIAL
YEARS SERV

Alderman Spooner, a colliery proprietor, was councillor for the north ward of the town. This plate disappeared from the centre pillar of the shelter by the lake in the 1960's and was found in the lake during its refurbishment in 1984.

QUEENS PARK, CHESTERFIELD.

The Queen's Park, with its old bandstand near the lake, in about 1907. This postcard, heavily retouched and rare, because of the Borough Arms, has been poorly printed in Bavaria. It does, though, convey a relaxed Sunday afternoon band concert atmosphere. It seems to be a hand-coloured copy of an earlier monochrome card by Waterhouse.

ORDER OF
PROCESSION
TO BE OBSERVED
ON WEDNESDAY, MAY 17, 1837,
ON OCCASION OF LAYING THE
FIRST STONE
OF THE
CHURCH OF THE HOLY TRINITY,
CHESTERFIELD.

TWO TRUMPETERS.
BANNER.   BANNER.
GIRLS WITH BASKETS OF FLOWERS.
TWO WHITE WANDS.
CHILDREN OF THE NATIONAL AND SUNDAY SCHOOLS, FOUR ABREAST.
TWO WHITE WANDS.
BENEFIT SOCIETIES, FOUR ABREAST.
BAND.
TWO WHITE WANDS.
GENTRY OF THE TOWN AND NEIGHBOURHOOD.
BANNER.
TWO WHITE WANDS.
THE ARCHITECT,
MASTER CARPENTER. { WITH PLANS AND INSCRIPTION PLATE. } MASTER MASON.
OTHER CONTRACTORS.
WORKMEN.
TWO WHITE WANDS.
COUNTY MAGISTRATES.
TWO WHITE WANDS.
MAYOR, ALDERMEN, AND COUNCIL OF THE BOROUGH, WITH THEIR MACE.
THE VICAR   { THE ARCHDEACON
OF CHESTERFIELD. } THE LORD LIEUTENANT OF THE COUNTY. { OF DERBY.
TWO WHITE WANDS.
THE TRUSTEES OF TRINITY CHURCH.
THE CLERGY, ROBED, TWO ABREAST.
CHURCHWARDENS OF CHESTERFIELD.
CHURCHWARDENS OF THE HAMLETS.
SIDESMEN OF CHESTERFIELD.

GENTLEMEN OF THE COMMITTEE (left margin)
GENTLEMEN OF THE COMMITTEE (right margin)

The Clubs from the Hamlets will assemble at the Town Hall, and the Chesterfield Clubs at their respective Club-rooms, by twelve o'clock. The Children of the Schools, and the Flower Girls, will assemble at the National School-room at that hour. At half-past twelve the Church Bell will Toll for five minutes, when it is requested that the several parties will proceed in bodies to the New Square, in order to take their places in the line of Procession; which will move to the site at one o'clock. As the Procession arrives, the several bodies will take the stations which shall then be pointed out to them. The Flower Girls will strew the internal Area of the Church with Flowers. The 100th Psalm will be Sung; after which the Silver Trowel will be presented by the Secretary of the Committee to His Grace the Duke of Devonshire, who will lay the Foundation Stone with due formalities; a Prayer will then be offered up by the Archdeacon of Derby; and an Address will be delivered by the Vicar of Chesterfield. A Hymn, composed for the occasion, will then be Sung; and the Benediction immediately following, will conclude the Ceremony.

THE HYMN, NEATLY PRINTED ON A TINTED CARD,
May be procured of the Booksellers.

Events of the kind advertised here were always accompanied by due pomp and ceremony, providing as they did a welcome diversion in many humdrum lives. They were invariably very well attended. The church cost £3,300 to build on land donated by the Duke of Devonshire, who laid the stone.

A great day in the history of Chesterfield, and for the man who was the inspiration behind many of the Company's developments. The scene in the Market Place, on June 22, 1897, the diamond jubilee of Queen Victoria. The central figure on the platform, in tricorne hat and chain of office, is C. P. Markham, who was to be Chief Citizen again in 1909 and 1910. The photograph was lent by Mr. C. Mather, the firm's Pensions Officer.

The Market Place in 1897, and the town centre *en fête* for the Queen's Jubilee celebrations. This picture is reproduced from the *Staveley News*, with the permission of its Editor, and includes the caption referring to its former Managing Director and the town's Mayor, Charles Paxton Markham. As a memorial of the Queen's Diamond Jubilee, a fund was set up and the Corporation provided land for the erection of a Drill Hall at the top of Goldwell Hill at Ashgate, later opened by Field Marshall Lord Roberts. This was pulled down in the early 1990's, and is now a car park.

Five
Commercial

High Street butcher in the 1890's. Samuel Redfern had a shop in Glumangate in 1872 before trading here at no. 8, and also at Holywell Street. Redfern carried on trading here as a grocer, as well as on High Street, next to Boots Chemists, well into the 1950's.

WILL URTON,

GLUMAN GATE, CHESTERFIELD,

MANUFACTURER OF

FILES, SAWS, EDGE TOOLS. &c., AND GENERAL MERCHANT.

Joiners' Edge and Engineers' Tools, Screw Stocks and Dies, Rack Braces, Drill Braces, Pulley Blocks, Cramps, &c., &c.. always in Stock; also a great variety of Chaff Cutters. Cake Breakers, Pulpers, Corn Crushers, Ploughs, &c.

Agent for all kinds of Agricultural Implements and Machinery, by the Best Makers of England and America.

ALL GOODS WARRANTED OF BEST QUALITY.

THOMAS PEARSON,
Plumber, Glazier, and Gas Fitter,

GLUMAN GATE, CHESTERFIELD.

Lead Pumps. Water Closets, Beer Machines, Zinc Spouting, &c.. fixed on the Best Principles, and on the most Reasonable Terms.

HARDY CUNDITH,
SADDLER AND LEGGING MANUFACTURER,
No. 4, Town Hall Buildings, Gluman Gate, Chesterfield,

Has constantly on hand a choice stock of

Hunting Saddles and Bridles. Sets of Brass and Silver Mounted Harness. Horse Covers. Rugs and Suits of Clothing. Portmanteaus, Carpet and Leather Bags.

Home-made Leggings.   A Challenge to the World.

Advertisements from the last century. Will Urton's shop was best known when he opened on West Bars, opposite the Portland Hotel. He also had a warehouse occupying much of Park Road. The business survived until the late 1950's, when the last Will Urton retired.

118

Harold Brummell and his wife Ada kept the small baker's shop on Beetwell Street for many years. Pictured is Mrs. Brummell outside the shop in about 1922, with her son, Phillip, who was drowned on war service in 1942.

Hadfield's Pork Butchers traded from 1859 to 1964. Founded by a Sam Hadfield, possibly on Lordsmill Street, it was the largest business of its kind in the town, and for many years operated a restaurant over the shop which was run by the family till closure. Another Samuel Hadfield was elected a councillor in 1910, becoming an Alderman; two of his sons, Frank in 1952 and Leslie in 1959, both served as Mayor.

Researchers of old Chesterfield have many reasons to be grateful to C.H. Nadin, the 'Son' on this sign. William Nadin, previously the butler to E.A.J. Maynard at West House on West Bars, where his wife was the housekeeper, ran the business shown with young Charles Harold. C.H. trained in basket-making and began practising photography in the 1890's, becoming very proficient. He took his camera to local events and recorded views of the town, producing them as postcards for sale in the shop, and also to local newspapers. He also reproduced his photographs as lantern slides and gave lectures in the area. He died in 1942 in his 70th year.

John Turner's shop in the early 1900's. Turner founded the business in 1845, this shop being on the corner of South Street, next to the Falcon Restaurant; the shops at the 5 and 9 Packer's Row premises were then established in addition to this one and later incorporated no. 7. When rebuilt in the half-timbered style in the early 1930's the shop shown was relinquished. The enterprise prospered as one of the leading suppliers of clothing and drapery before a takeover by Courtauld and closure in 1987, when all but the façade was demolished.

Generations of cyclists must have known and been helped by George Curtois in his shop in Brampton. The small shop, on the site of a long-gone beer house, was occupied in 1931, George buying the good will for the sum of £12. He built up and ran the business until his death in 1978 aged 80.

Scales & Salter, later Scales & Son, were in business on the corner of High Street and Glumangate from before 1872 to the 1900's, in what had once been the Town Hall. The china and glass shop of Mrs. Pilley traded under that name into the 1950's.

Crossley Mitchell, trading as 'The Cash Butcher', had a shop in St. Helen's Street in 1895 when this photograph was taken. He also sold meat wholesale round the district in his smart horse-drawn van. Beef at $3\frac{1}{2}$d. per pound sounds good – but after hanging about in the open air all day?

J. T. BOOTH,
THE TEA ESTABLISHMENT, TOP OF THE MARKET-PLACE, CHESTERFIELD.
NEW CROP TEAS!!!

J. T. B. calls special attention to his stock of NEW TEAS of this year's growth, and would remark that the same personal care and attention will be taken in the selection and blending of his Teas which has gained for them such general preference, and that his customers may always depend upon BOOTH's Teas continuing to be, as heretofore, THE BEST.

BLACK TEAS.

Strong Congou............. 1s. 8d. & 2s. 0d.	Our Choicest Mixture of the
Strong Useful Congou 2s. 4d. & 2s. 8d.	Finest Flavoured Teas .... 4s. 0d.
Superior Congou .... 3s. 0d.	Strong Tea Dust .... 1s. 6d.
Rich Flavoured, recommended ... 3s. 4d.	Finest Tea Dust........................ 2s. 6d.
High Class Tea .... 3s. 6d. & 3s. 8d.	

The Teas quoted above can be had mixed with Green, at the same prices.

GREEN TEA from 1s. 6d. per lb. to 5s. per lb.

TERMS CASH.—2d. per lb. off on parcels of 4lbs. and upwards. Carriage paid on boxes of 14lbs. No charge for boxes. Samples sent per post on application. General Order for Groceries to the Amount of 40s. Carriage paid.

☞ Observe the Address, as above, NEXT DOOR BUT ONE TO
Mr. T. P. WOOD'S VAULTS.

Agent for the Litre Bottle Wine Company. The Litre Bottle holds 25 per cent. more than the "reputed quart." Claret from 12s. per doz. litre bottles; Rousillon or French Port 20s. 6d.; Golden Sherry (excellent dinner wine) 22s. 6d.; Port 22s. 6d. and 28s. 6d. per doz. litre bottles.

As the pointing finger in the advertisement indicates, J.T. Booth's Tea and Coffee shop stood on the High Street in the Market Place on the site now used by Marks & Spencer and may be seen in many pictures of that area. Booth traded from the middle 1800's into the twentieth century.

124

Herbert Green established his tobacco retail and wholesale business at no. 1 Holywell Street on the corner of Tapton Lane in the late 1870's, and it was carried on by his family until the retirement of the last proprietor, Robert Green, a well-known and popular figure in the town, in the 1970's.

The Hippodrome, c. 1920, with flagpole and gas lighting. This building, originally known as the Theatre Royal, replaced an earlier theatre of about 1900 and showed silent films until 1930, when a talking film with Buster Keaton and Jack Benny was shown. The theatre was controlled by Terence Byrom Ltd. in the mid-30's and continued with live variety shows, seasonal circuses and pantomimes, often featuring well-known artistes, before closing in 1954.

R.J. Stokes, the Sheffield-based firm, established a presence in the town at no. 15 in the old Knifesmithgate, next to the Mallet & Tool public house, in the 1900's. They stayed more or less in this position, becoming possibly the oldest inhabitants under the 'Vic Arches', until closure in 1994.

The hairdressing salon of Reginald Geo. Boult at no.7 Holywell Street in about 1920, where a child's hair could be cut and singed for 2½p. Boult's daughter, May, carried on the business for some time into the 1940's.

126

Alfred Seaman came to the town in 1886, establishing a small photographic business from a wooden hut on the corner of Tapton Lane and Brewery Street, later moving to the shop at the top of the lane opposite the Memorial Hall. Alfred then moved to Sheffield to open a shop on London Road there, but his sons returned to the town and opened a shop on High Street, near the church, later moving to their well-known premises further along High Street. The business moved in 1926 to premises in Irongate which had been an inn, the Durham Ox, until 1977, when they moved to first floor premises in the same area, eventually closing this in 1988. The business still continues from a private address. This shot shows the firm during its short occupation of the corner of the Market Hall, with window dressing, possibly for a shopping festival. Seamans were perhaps the first choice of portrait photography for over half a century and pioneered several novel techniques.

This spectacularly dressed window was the work of William Denham Bales at his tool and ironmonger's business at 17 Burlington Street, in front of the old Picture Palace cinema. The window was probably entered for the competition run in the 1912 Shopping Festival.

As with the Midland Hotel behind it, Freemans Temperance Hotel was sited to benefit from the nearby railway station. Photographed in around 1905, this queerly-shaped building had been enlarged by Freeman, and had fourteen en-suite bedrooms, two dining rooms and two billiard rooms. It was demolished in 1983 for the inner relief road to pass directly beneath the site.

Figaro was a scurrilous and radical weekly pamphlet published and printed by Thomas Ford, a stationer in New Square in 1832. The editor was thought to have been H. Adams, who was paid by the Pikes who then owned a shop on Low Pavement and ran a Derby newspaper, possibly the *Derby & Chesterfield Reporter*. *Figaro* gloried in attacking the public figures of the day, especially politicians, both local and national, and even the Church.

William Burkitt's maltster business was based in Saltergate before 1870, supplying malt and hops to many ale-houses in the town and around. He also imported grain to the town and to his firm in Langwith through his depot in King's Lynn. This 1890's picture shows a delivery dray after his sons, William and Samuel, had taken over. Sam then lived at Stubbing Court.

Horns Bridge and Lordsmill Street in the 1970's. Demolition had started on the east side of the road and the premises opposite have been abandoned. Through the arch can be seen the Chesterfield Cylinders' Alma Works, the closure of which was announced in 1994. Wragg's motor-cycle business, having replaced the long-established Jervis Brothers, has moved to Whittington Moor.

Six

Transport

The first horse-drawn tram ran as a private enterprise, on 4ft. 8½in. gauge, from Brampton Terminus to the Market Hall on Low Pavement from 1882. In 1886 it was taken over by twelve local businessmen who increased the number of cars from three to five. In 1897 the Corporation bought out the Chesterfield Tramways for £2,050, operating it until electrification in 1904. This restored sixteen-seat car was built in 1899 for one-horse operation and was photographed at Crich Museum.

A double-decker on Lower Chatsworth Road in the 1890's. These cars were made by Ashbury's of Manchester on a patent chassis by Eades. At the termini the horses side-stepped from front to rear, turning the car on the chassis, thus avoiding unharnessing them. When these trams became Corporation-owned the livery was a smart Prussian blue and primrose.

Hansom cabs await customers from the Angel Hotel, c. 1905. Perhaps some of these early 'taxis' came from Paulson's livery around the corner in Soresby Street, or from Charles Fisher on Holywell Street, both well-known cab proprietors.

Knifesmithgate in about 1900, later named Stephenson Place, in honour of George. In these days this was, via Holywell Street and Corporation Street, the main route to the Midland Station. Here an empty dray is proceeding in a leisurely manner back for more goods.

Open-top car no. 9 on High Street, by the Market Place, in the early tram period around 1907. The extra trade on market days was thought to make this narrow street unsafe for trams and they were reversed by the Market Hall and Stephenson Place to return to Brampton and Whittington.

Another open-top car, stationary on Burlington Street, i.e. not a Market Day. To the left of the frame is J.K. Swallows' early store with its gas lamps, and opposite is the beehive sign outside the draper's shop of Charles Shaw, who was reputed to sleep frequently under his own counter.

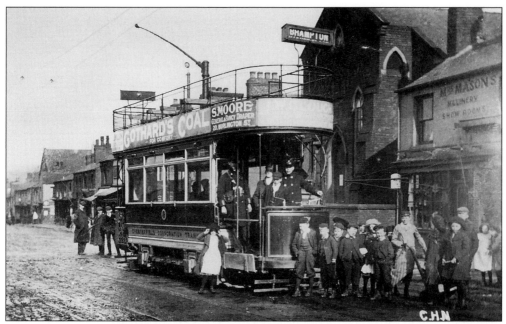

Tramcar no.7 at the Whittington Moor Terminus, with the usual crowd of onlookers attendant on many photographic occasions. Notice the elaborate iron gate on the rear platform and the state of the road on the left.

An early Corporation bus, a Tilling-Stevens, wearing its relatively new livery of green and cream, outside the then Yorkshire Penny Bank on Central Pavement in 1926. The driver shown is Joseph Henry Sergeant, who had also driven the electric trams, and his cheerful conductress was Annie Revill (later Elliott) of Chester Street, who lived to be over one hundred years old.

This bus had a war record: the body was built in Lowestoft, put on an ex-army AEC-Y lorry chassis and leased to W.T. Underwood Ltd. of Clowne. Licensed by Chesterfield Corporation, this 32-seater plied between the town and Barrowhill from 1921-26. The driver and conductress are unknown, but Underwood's company name became the East Midland's in 1927.

One of the early Straker-Clough single-decked trolley buses, seen at the new Thornfield depot on Sheffield Road in the 1920's, possibly for a demonstration run for Committee members. These buses gave good economical service on Brampton–Whittington routes to March 1938 and were financially successful, even though outnumbered by petrol-engined vehicles on other Corporation routes.

The old and the new at Stephenson Place in May 1927: a Bristol bus makes ready for its journey to Brampton, whilst No.7 tramcar has its pick-up boom reversed prior to going the other way to Whittington. The Bristol was only temporarily on this route during the highway conversion from trams to trolley buses.

Our policemen are so obliging, especially to the Mayor Ald. C.P. Markham on Coronation Day in 1910, when he visited the schools wearing his robes of office. The mace bearer seems to be hiding a smile as the P.C. is trying to start the engine outside the Victoria School, Vicar Lane.

The beginning of a trip from the Bricklayer's Arms in South Street in the 1920's, the later '20's to judge from the pneumatic tyres on the charabanc. An outing meant 'out' in those days, whatever the weather, with only a canvas hood for protection.

An early minibus? Horses are still catered for, judging by the presence of the pump and trough outside the Devonshire Arms at Hasland in about 1905. There are pneumatics on this converted car (is it a Renault?) but no windscreen. One wonders what the small boy on the left is up to!

One of the impressive steam lorries used by the Brampton Brewery on its delivery round in the 1920's and early '30's. The Brewery, largest of the three in the town, was built near the Holmbrook between Wheatbridge Road and Chatsworth Road some time before 1839 and at the time of its takeover by Warwicks in 1955, owned 116 public houses.

This photograph, from the early 1930's or just before, was taken to mark the completion of the bodywork on Townrow's lorry by the firm of Marsden Brothers. Marsden's was founded by three brothers from Birchover in the Toch H Yard, Brampton, part of the family later operating from Hardwick's Yard. In the picture are (left to right) Wm. Marsden Snr., Wm. Marsden Jnr., Alfred Marsden, Mr. Parker (joiner), Mr. Landers (signwriter) and Mr. Shawcross (blacksmith).

One of the Scarsdale Brewery's magnificent 1920's delivery wagons posed in Hollis Lane, very near to the works. Unfortunately, neither the chain-driven lorry nor its attendants have been identified. Brewing was first carried out on Spa Lane in 1822 by T. Tallent, and the name of the then owners, J.&F. Dunnell, is carved on the stone pediment of the vaults on St. Mary's Gate. The business was owned and run variously by Eyre and J.B. White (late of High Street) but became the Scarsdale Brewery Ltd. in 1865, when the preserved offices facing Vicar Lane were opened as the Scarsdale Hotel. Battling through cash difficulties and a bankruptcy in 1878, the business was acquired by Thomas I. Birkin for £42,750 and thrived under the Birkins until a takeover by Whitbread's in 1958. Brewing ceased in 1959 and the premises were bought by the Corporation, all but the vaults and offices being demolished in 1961.

This trim new delivery lorry – thought to be a Commer – pictured in Pipe Lane, now Middlecroft Road, in 1926, was owned by Kendal & Elliott, the well-known mineral water manufacturers in Staveley. The young lady in the cab was Miss Mabel Elliott, the daughter of the proprietor, who took over the business in 1921. He died in 1962 and the Company was sold in 1965.

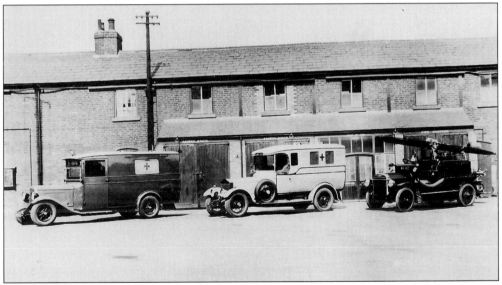

The Staveley Company's emergency service vehicles in 1926. Previously comprising the Austin ambulance, and the newly acquired Dennis fire engine, the service was augmented in July 1926 by the presentation, by the late Chairman's widow Mrs. Markham, of the chassis of her husband's Rolls Royce. This was fitted with an ambulance body by T. Metcalfe of Chesterfield and was used for many years by the company.

The modern age of Chesterfield Corporation transport in 1937. A new Leyland Tiger single-decker waits at Elder Way for passengers to Barlow Commonside. These new diesel-engined buses proved far more economical to run than the petrol-engined Bristol 'B' types and were the pattern for the future. It is not generally known that four Regent double-decked buses were lent to London Transport in 1940-41 to replace those lost in the blitz.

A rare photograph showing a scene never now to be repeated: a 1950's view of two railways taken from a third. The left to right line is the LMS, and under the footbridge can be seen the LNER loop line going under the Brampton Spur before entering the Hollis Lane Bridge. On the left is the Horn's Bridge signal box and the Horn's Hotel.

The Midland Railway had its own architect, Neill, who designed this station in the Gothic style for G.F. Kirk to build in the 1870's. It was pictured here in about 1907, together with a fine selection of bowler hats, boaters and elegant carriages.

Market Place station in the tramcar days, probably the early 1920's. Conceived initially by William Arkwright of Sutton Scarsdale as a direct line from Warrington, on the Manchester Ship Canal, to new docks to be built at Sutton-on-Sea, the project, started in 1892, ran into financial difficulties in 1894. This forced a curtailment of the plan, and the Lancashire Derbyshire and East Coast Railway only ever ran from Chesterfield to Pyewipe Junction, near Lincoln, and after a takeover of the company in 1907 by the Great Central, which ran it as a local service, the line closed in 1957.

The Great Central station was the second in Chesterfield and was opened in 1892 by the Manchester, Sheffield and Lincolnshire Railway Company, which was acquired by the GC in 1897. The line through Chesterfield was not a main route but a loop, branching from the main line near Heath and rejoining it at Staveley. This charming station closed for ever in September 1967 and the town's by-pass now runs along almost the same route.

Seven

Districts

This charming scene is in fact Longedge Lane at Wingerworth in the early 1900's. The house behind the tree is said to have been the laundry of nearby Wingerworth Hall, the home of the Hunloke family.

Hartington Road, Spital in the 1920's, looking much the same as it does today. The district derived its name from a leper hospital sited a few hundred yards to the north in the 12th century. The hospital was dedicated to St. Leonard, who tended the sick, and this is still part of the St. Leonard's Ward of the town.

High Street, Staveley in the early 1900's. The largest building in the photograph, with an apparent spire, is the Markham Hall, named after C.P. Markham who, through developing the Staveley Company, brought prosperity to the area. Advertising on the house wall was for Nestles, Gunstones and Eyre & Sons – all extant in 1994.

The Oxford Picture House, New Whittington, in the 1920's. This cinema operated throughout the war and gave its final showing in June 1956.

The White Hart, Walton in about 1912. Could the lady in the doorway be the licensee, Hannah Taylor? That part to the left of centre was the old pub and the rest was an addition in 1904 by the owners, Brampton Brewery.

South Street, New Whittington. A photograph by Crowther-Cox of about 1900. Most photographs in public places attracted onlookers at this time, but this number appears exceptional – even the pony and trap are prepared to wait.

Tapton House in 1970. This late-Georgian mansion on Castle Hill, to the north of the town, was leased by the owner, Isaac Wilkinson, to George Stephenson, who died in the house and was buried in Trinity Church. It was then sold to Charles Markham, who married Rosa Paxton; their son, Charles Paxton Markham, then living at Ringwood Hall, gave the house and grounds to the town in 1925. It became a co-educational school in 1931.

The Cotton Mill at Holymoorside in the early 1900's. Although built in the late 1700's, it came to its peak under the ownership of Simeon Manlove, who had started cotton spinning in Nottingham. He built up the business from the 1840's, later using steam motive power rather than water from the Hipper and the mill dam. Manlove's sons ran the mill till 1897, when they sold it to the English Sewing Cotton Co. Ltd., who closed it in 1905. Used as an army camp (1914-1918) and rest home for Markham Works employees, it was finally demolished by 1927.

Old Whittington, c. 1900 A view of the Revolution House by Crowther Cox, an excellent photographer from Rotherham who seemed to work mostly around Whittington and Staveley. Once an ale-house called the Cock & Pynot (magpie), it was the venue in 1688 of a meeting between conspirators when the Earls of Devonshire and Danby and John d'Arcy discussed their schemes which later that year removed James II from the throne of England. William of Orange, with his wife, Mary (daughter of James II), took his place by invitation. The cottage has been a museum since the 1930s.

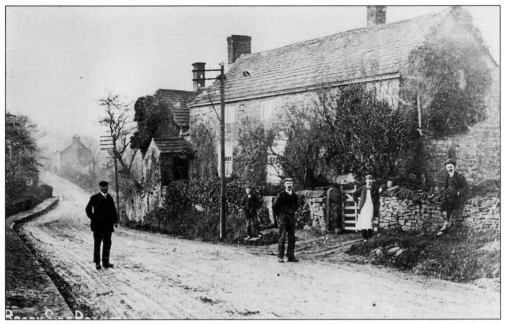

Brookside, Brampton, about the turn of the century. This house may have been the Royal Oak public house (previously the Appletree Inn), last mentioned in Trade Directories in 1852.

Dunston Lane in the 1940s. The group of houses – all having postal addresses in Dunston Lane – near to Littlemoor, were completed before the outbreak of war in 1939. Further development of the area did not begin till the 1950-60 period.

Church Lane, Old Whittington, about 1895. An interesting group by Crowther Cox, of which some names are known. Left to right: Mr. Tims, Lois Tims, Mr. Tims, Snr. The next lady is Mrs. Bargh, with her daughter, and the man apart, nearest the church, is Tom Moxon, the mason who carved the Joseph Syddall-designed three-dimensional cross on the war memorial near the Revolution House.

Eight
Aerial Views

The southern aspect of the town in the late 1920's. Notice the houses of Church Alley, bottom left, and the many small dwellings to the east of the church.

The view from the west in 1928. There are not many vehicles to be seen here on a sunny midday but shop blinds seem to be popular.

The Devonshire Works of the Staveley Coal & Iron Company in the 1940s. Charles Paxton Markham was the architect of these works on land leased from the Duke of Devonshire, north of the Rother. It embodied, at this time, four blast furnaces, one hundred and seventy coke ovens and many chemical plants converting the by-products.

The Derby Road in the 1930s. The plant known locally as the 'Tube Works', now Chesterfield Cylinders, is on the right, and the unfinished St. Augustine estate is upper left.

155

Items of interest in this 1940s photograph are the chimney and gasholder (bottom left) of the Midland Railway Company gasworks (see p. 12), and the old silk mill on Markham Road which was demolished in the 1960s.

In this view, taken from the tower of the Crooked Spire in the 1940s, the old LMS station, the Hippodrome and most of Corporation Street can be seen. There are also three hotels and one ex-hotel in the frame: the Station, the Clifton, the Midland and the furniture shop which used to be Freeman's Temperance Hotel. It had a tight little community in the yard behind it.

The north of the town in the 1950s, and a chance to see how many dwelling houses have disappeared from between Holywell Street and Brewery Street since that time.

Another photograph from the church tower, showing a scene very different from 1994. All the block between Saltergate and Holywell Street and all the dwelling houses behind the Primitive Methodist Chapel have gone.

Some of the major changes in the town since the war have been to the south: in the 1940s the Lordsmill Street area looked like this. Progress has seen the removal of almost all the buildings below Vicar Lane and to the west of the edge of the picture, including three fine pubs, the Crown, the Prince of Wales and the Black Bull Inn.